Bernd Römmelt

Fünfseenland
und Pfaffenwinkel

Bernd Römmelt

Fünfseenland und Pfaffenwinkel

Traumblicke im Münchner Süden

rosenheimer

Inhalt

Contents

Eine Annäherung

Nur 20 Kilometer südlich von München beginnt ein Gebiet, das man kurzum als Oberbayern par excellence beschreiben kann: das Fünfseenland, und ein Stückchen weiter südlich der Pfaffenwinkel. Beide Gebiete sind fast untrennbar miteinander verbunden. Teile des südlichen Starnberger und Ammersees gehören historisch eigentlich schon zum Pfaffenwinkel, geografisch aber zum Fünfseenland. Beide Landstriche kenne ich seit meiner Kindheit und habe sie ins Herz geschlossen.

Das Fünfseenland umfasst zwei größere Seen, zwei kleinere und einen Winzling. Starnberger See, Ammersee, Wörthsee, Pilsensee und Weßlinger See buhlen an heißen Sommertagen um die Gunst der Badegäste – vor allem aus der Landeshauptstadt. Denn von München sind es auf der Autobahn A 95 nur rund 20 Kilometer bis zur Ausfahrt nach Starnberg, und nach weiteren 5 Kilometern ist der Ort Starnberg und damit das nördliche Ende des Starnberger Sees erreicht. Bleibt man auf der A 95 und fährt noch einmal 20 Kilometer bis zur Ausfahrt Seeshaupt, dann gelangt man zum Südende des Sees. Wer von München an den Ammersee oder einen seiner drei Trabanten will, der fährt auf der Lindauer Autobahn 25 Kilometer Richtung Westen. Sowohl Starnberger als auch Ammersee sind also Seen des Alpenvorlandes. Zwischen sanften Hügeln liegen sie wie Perlen im Land vor den Bergen. Im Süden erhebt sich mächtig das Zugspitzmassiv, und an Föhntagen rückt die Alpenkette zum Greifen nahe.

Die südlichen Enden des Starnberger und Ammersees gehören, wie gesagt, eigentlich schon zum Pfaffenwinkel. Diesen grenzt im Osten die Loisach vom Tölzer Land, im Westen der Lech vom Allgäu ab. Das Murnauer Moos im Süden bil-

det den sanften Übergang zum bergigen Werdenfelser Land. Natürlich sind dies keine Grenzen im eigentlichen Sinn, doch gerade der Pfaffenwinkel hat eine ganz eigene, besondere Ausstrahlung, und für mich ist er das Herz Oberbayerns. Vieles, was man mit dieser schönsten unter den deutschen Landschaften verbindet, findet man hier so konzentriert an wie nirgendwo sonst. Wo etwa gibt es so viele Klöster, Kirchen und Kapellen wie zwischen Lech und Loisach? Der prachtvolle Ritt zu Ehren des heiligen Leonhard, die vielen großen und kleinen Fronleichnams- oder Maria-Himmelfahrts-Prozessionen sind hier noch nicht zum Touristenspektakel verkommen, sondern Ausdruck eines tief in den Menschen verwurzelten Glaubens. Angulus sacerdotum, Priester- oder eben Pfaffenwinkel – dieses Land trägt seinen Namen zu Recht. Berühmte Klöster und Kirchen wie Wessobrunn, Benediktbeuern oder die prachtvolle Rokoko-Wallfahrtskirche »zum Gegeißelten Heiland auf der Wies« sind auch heute noch Pilgerorte für Menschen aus nah und fern.

Auch manche Künstler hat der Paffenwinkel angezogen. So entdeckte Franz Marc »das blaue Land« zwischen Kochel und Murnau für sich und ließ sich von der Landschaft inspirieren. Auch Gabriele Münter und Wassily Kandinsky lebten und wirkten in Murnau, dem Zentrum des Landes.

Die Schönheiten des Pfaffenwinkels erschließt man sich am besten zu Fuß. Anmutige Seen wie die Osterseen, der Staffelsee, Riegsee und Kochelsee schmiegen sich zwischen die sanften Hügel des Alpenvorlandes. Eine Vielzahl von Naturschutzgebieten lädt zum Wandern und Staunen ein. Ein Spaziergang durch das Kochel- oder Murnauer Moos etwa lässt das Herz eines jeden Naturliebhabers höher schlagen. Auch große Teile des Staffelsees und der Osterseen stehen unter Schutz und beheimaten eine Vielzahl seltener Pflanzen- und Tierarten.

Herbst am Staffelsee
Autumn on Lake Staffelsee

An Approach

A region that could be described as real Upper Bavaria begins just 20 km south of Munich: the Land of the Five Lakes, and a little farther south is Pfaffenwinkel. The two are almost inseparably linked; parts of the southern Lake Starnberg and Lake Ammersee in fact belong historically to Pfaffenwinkel but geographically to the Five Lakes region. I have known both areas since my childhood and am very fond of them.

The Five Lakes consist of two larger, two smaller and one tiny lake. On hot summer days, Lake Starnberg, Lake Worthsee, Lake Pilsen and Lake Wessling compete for the attention of bathers, chiefly from Munich. From the capital of Bavaria it is just 20 km along the A95 highway to the exit for Starnberg and another 5 km to the town of Starnberg at the northern end of the lake. If you stay on the A95 for another 20 km you reach the exit for Seeshaupt and the southern end of the lake.

In order to get to the Lake Ammersee or one of its three "satellites", you drive 25 km westwards along the Lindau Autobahn. Both, Lake Starnberg and Lake Ammersee, are in the foothills of the Alps, and are located between gentle hills, like beads, against the backdrop of the mountains. The mighty Zugspitze mass rises up in the south and on days, when the infamous warm, dry wind called Foehn blows, the mountain range seems near enough to reach out and touch.

The southern ends of Lake Starnberg and Lake Ammersee actually belong, as mentioned above, to Pfaffenwinkel, which is bordered by the river Loisach in the east from the Bad Tolz area and the river Lech in the west, from the Allgau region. The Murnau Moos (moorland) in the south crosses over gently to the mountainous Werdenfels region. These are not real borders, of course, but Pfaffenwinkel radiates something special and peculiar to itself and constitutes the very heart of Oberbayern (Upper Bavaria), as far as I am concerned. Much of what one associates with the most beautiful of the German countryside is to be found concentrated here like nowhere else. Where can you see as many monasteries, churches and chapels as there are between the rivers Lech and Loisach? The splendid Ritt (procession) in honour of St. Leonhard, or the many greater and smaller processions on Corpus Christi and the Dormition of the Virgin have not disintegrated into shows for the tourists, but are the genuine expression of people's profound faith. Whether Angelus sacerdotum, "Priests' Corner" or Pfaffenwinkel – this region rightly bears its name. The famous monasteries and churches like Wessobrunn, Benediktbeuren or the splendid rococco Pilgrimage Church of the Scourged Saviour ("zum Gegeisselten Heiland auf der Wies") are still visited by pilgrims from all over.

Pfaffenwinkel has also attracted artists: Franz Marc discovered "the Blue Land" between Kochel and Murnau and became inspired by the scenery. Gabriele Münter and Vassily Kandinsky lived and painted in Murnau, the lively centre of the area.

The beauty of Pfaffenwinkel is best appreciated on foot. Charming lakes like the Osterseen (Easter Lakes), Lake Staffelsee, Lake Riegsee and Lake Kochelsee nestle in the gentle foothills of the alps. The many nature reserves are inviting for hikers, and a walk through the Kochel and Murnau moors delights and amazes nature lovers. Greater parts of Lake Staffelsee and the Easter Lakes are home to many rare plants and animal species which are protected.

Die geschützte Trollblume im Murnauer Moos
The protected globe flower on the Murnau Moss

Sonnenuntergang über dem Starnberger See nahe St. Heinrich
Sunset over Lake Starnberg near St. Heinrich

Morgennebel im Kochelmoos
Morning mist on the Kochelmoos

Blick von der Aidlinger Höhe auf die
Zugspitze
View from the Aidlinger Hill to the
Zugspitze

Was wäre der Pfaffenwinkel ohne seine Marterl!
What is Pfaffenwinkel without its wayside crosses!

Verzaubertes Kochelmoos
Enchanted Kochelmoos ➜

Pferdeschmuck »der anderen Art« beim Leonhardi-Ritt in Benediktbeuern
Another kind of horse decoration at the St. Leonhard's Ride in Benediktbeuern

Leonhardi-Ritt in Benediktbeuern
St. Leonhard's Ride in Benediktbeuern

← *Blick über das Freilichtmuseum auf der Glentleiten hinweg auf das nebelverhangene Kochelmoos*
View over the Openair Museum Glentleiten and across the Kochelmoos, shrouded in mist

Kloster Andechs erstarrt in Kälte
Andechs Monastery numbed with cold

Stillleben in Kochel
Still life in Kochel

Prächtig geschmückte Balkone und Gärten in Bernried am Starnberger See
Splendidly decorated balconies and gardens in Bernried on Lake Starnberg

19

Rund um das Kochelmoos

Wer sich früh morgens von München auf der Autobahn A 95 Richtung Süden aufmacht, der wird wahrscheinlich spätestens ab der Ausfahrt Sindelsdorf im Nebel stecken. Grund dafür ist das Kochelmoos. Einst lag hier der große Rohrsee, der jedoch trockengelegt wurde. Mehrere wunderschöne Wege führen durch das Gebiet, gesäumt von kleinen Heuschobern. Aber aufgepasst, die Wege dürfen zwischen April und Juli nicht verlassen werden, da der große Brachvogel, ein scheuer Wiesenbrüter, zu dieser Zeit seine Jungen aufzieht. Wer Glück hat, kann im Mai und Juni den Fuchsnachwuchs beim Spielen auf den Wiesen beobachten.

Schon von weitem sichtbar, erheben sich im äußersten Osten des Mooses zwei Zwiebeltürme in den Himmel. Kloster Benediktbeuern, das älteste Kloster Bayerns, liegt direkt am Rand des Moorgebietes. 740 gründeten Benediktinermönche im Ort Beuern ein Kloster, aus Beuern wurde Benediktbeuern, aus der Bergwand mit dem Zackenkamm im Rücken des Klosters die Benediktenwand. Die Benediktiner mehrten ihre Güter im weiten Umkreis, und das Kloster wurde zum reichsten im ganzen Oberland. Heute wird die weitläufige Barockanlage von Salesianern Don Boscos geführt, die eine Philosophisch-Theologische Hochschule aufbauten. Berühmt sind die kulturellen Veranstaltungen, wie Lesungen und Konzerte.

Ein Stück weiter südlich gelangt man nach Kochel. Vor dem Gasthof zur Post steht das Denkmal des Schmieds von Kochel. Er soll sich beim Aufstand der Oberlandler besonders hervorgetan haben, die 1705 in einem Verzweiflungsakt versuchten, München und Oberbayern von der Österreichischen Besatzung zu befreien, und in der »Sendlinger Mordweihnacht« am 25. Dezember 1705 grausam niedergemetzelt wurden.

Morgenrot über dem Eichensee im Kochelmoos
Sunrise over the Lake Eichensee in Kochelmoos

Kochel hat jedoch nicht nur seinen Schmied. Dem Künstler Franz Marc, der zeitweilig im nahen Ried lebte, wurde ein ganzes Museum gewidmet. Wem der Sinn nicht nach Kunst steht, der kann im »Trimini« direkt am Ufer des Kochelsees die Vorzüge eines modernen Erlebnisbads genießen.

Hoch über Kochel ist eine Meisterleistung bayerischer Ingenieurskunst zu bewundern: das Walchenseekraftwerk. Im kohlearmen Oberbayern bot es sich an, die Wasserkraft zur Stromgewinnung zu nutzen. Der berühmte Oskar von Miller wurde damit beauftragt, eine landesweite Stromversorgung aufzubauen. Ihn bewog die außergewöhnliche Natursituation, dass der Walchensee 200 Meter höher als der Kochelsee liegt, zum Bau eines Kraftwerks, das dieses Gefälle nutzt und zu den größten Ingenieursleistungen der frühen Zwanzigerjahre des letzten Jahrhunderts zählt. Sechs gewaltige Druckrohre von zwei Metern Durchmesser leiten das Wasser den Hang hinab zum Turbinenhaus am Südufer des Kochelsees, wo es die Generatoren antreibt. Der Wasserverbrauch ist so hoch, dass im Frühjahr und im Winter der Spiegel des Walchensees bis zu sechs Meter absinken kann.

Fährt man von Kochel Richtung Westen – im Süden immer Herzogstand und Heimgarten im Blickfeld – dann gelangt man nach wenigen Kilometern in den kleinen Ort Schlehdorf mit seinem mächtigen Kloster. Etwas oberhalb des Ortes befindet sich das Freilichtmuseum Glentleiten. Dort wurden seit 1973 über 46 historisch kostbare Höfe aus dem gesamten oberbayerischen Raum wieder errichtet, das heißt, von ihrem ursprünglichen Standort hierher verfrachtet und dann Balken für Balken neu aufgebaut. In Gruppen stehen die Höfe in der Landschaft, umgeben von den dazugehörigen Nebengebäuden: Backofen, Austragshäusl, Kapelle und Brunnen. Besondere Beachtung verdienen die liebevoll gestalteten Bauerngärten und die sorgfältige Innenausstattung der Häuser.

Around Kochelmoos

When you set off southwards in the early morning on the A95 from Munich you are bound to get stuck in fog by the time you reach the exit for Sindelsdorf. This is because of the Kochelmoos. There used to be a large lake here – Lake Rohrsee – but it was dried out. Many lovely paths lead through the region, lined with small haystacks. But watch out! Between April and July do not stray from the paths because the shy curlew rears its young at this time. If you are lucky, you can observe the offspring of foxes playing in the meadows in May and June. Two onion domes can be seen from afar in the sky to the extreme east of the Moor. Benediktbeuern, the oldest monastery of Bavaria, is on the edge of the moorland area. Benedictine monks founded a monastery in the place called Beuern in the year 740 and it became known as Benediktbeuern; the mountain face behind with jagged ridge became the Benedictine face. The monks increased the property all around and the monastery became the richest in the whole uplands area. Nowadays the spacious baroque building has been taken over by the Salesian Order of Don Boscos which set up a philosophical, theological college there and is famous for its cultural events such as readings and concerts.

A little further south is Kochel. In front of the inn "Gasthof zur Post" is the statue of the Blacksmith of Kochel who is supposed to have distinguished himself during a rebellion of uplanders who attempted in 1705 to liberate Munich and Upper Bavaria from Austrian occupation in an act of desperation, and who were cruelly butchered on December 25, 1705 in the "Sendling Christmas Massacre". But Kochel does not just boast its blacksmith. The artist Franz Marc, who lived temporarily in nearby Ried, has a whole museum dedicated to him. If culture does not interest you, perhaps you can enjoy the advantages of a modern water park on the shores of Lake Kochel.

High above Kochel a masterpiece of Bavarian engineering can be admired – the Walchensee Power Station. Since Upper Bavaria did not have much coal, it lent itself to utilise water power for the production of electricity. The famous Oscar von Miller was commissioned to set up a national electricity supply. He made use of the extraordinary situation provided by nature in that the lake of Walchensee lies 200 m above Lake Kochelsee, to build a power station using this downward slope and it counts as one of the greatest feats of engineering in the early twenties of the last century. Six enormous pressure tubes, two metres in diameter, pipe the water down the slope to the turbine plant on the southern shore of Lake Kochelsee to drive the generators. The water consumption is so great that in spring and winter the level of the Lake Walchensee can sink by six meters.

If you travel west of Kochel, keeping Herzogstand and Heimgarten in sight to the south, after a few kilometers you reach the village of Schlehdorf with its huge monastery. Above the village is the open-air museum of Glentleiten. Since 1973 more than 46 historically valuable farms have been reconstructed here from the entire Upper Bavarian region, that is to say, shipped here from their original location and rebuilt beam by beam. The farmhouses stand in groups in the countryside, surrounded by the buildings that belong next to them: oven, granny cottage, chapel and well. The lovingly tended country gardens and careful interiors of the houses are noteworthy.

Im Sommer eine Augenweide: die Bauerngärten im Freilichtmuseum auf der Glentleiten
A feast for the eyes in summer: country gardens at the Glentleiten Openair Museum

← *Nur langsam lichtet sich der Nebel über dem Kochelmoos.*
The mist clears very slowly over the Kochelmoos.

Nach einem heftigen Sommergewitter erstrahlt ein Regenbogen über Benediktbeuern.
Rainbow over Benediktbeuern after a summer thunderstorm

Skeptische Blicke beim Maibaumaufstellen in Kochel
Setting up the maypole in Kochel

Fronleichnamsprozession in Benedikt-
beuern (oben und unten)
Corpus Christi procession in Benedikt-
beuern (above and below)

Kloster Schlehdorf »spitzt« durch den Nebel
Schlehdorf monastery pointing through the mist

Kloster Benediktbeuern vor der prachtvollen Kulisse von Herzogstand und Heimgarten
Benediktbeuern Monastery in the splendid setting of Herzogstand and Heimgarten

Ein Wintermärchen an der Loisach
A winter fairytale on the river Loisach

Ein Heuschober im Kochelmoos, im Hintergrund der Jochberg
A barn on the Kochelmoos, Jochberg in the background ➜

Fliegenfischen an der Loisach
Fly-fishing at the Loisach

*»Der Schmied von Kochel«, ein ober-
bayerischer Held*
*"The Blacksmith of Kochel", a hero of
Bavaria*

Die Autobahn München–Garmisch-Partenkirchen führt wie ein Lindwurm am Kochelmoos vorbei. Im Hintergrund die Zugspitze
The Munich–Garmisch-Partenkirchen highway skirts the Kochelmoos like a lindworm. Zugspitze in the background

Walchenseekraftwerk, Kloster Schlehdorf, Karwendel, Herzogstand, Heimgarten
The Walchensee Power Station, Schlehdorf Monastery, Karwendel, Herzogstand and Heimgarten mountains ➜

← *Ein »magischer« Morgen im Moos. Vorne spitzt der Kirchturm von Ried heraus.*
Morning magic on the moss. Ried Church tower in the foreground

An manchen Tagen lichtet sich der Nebel überhaupt nicht; hier behält die Sonne zum Glück die Oberhand.
Sometimes the fog does not clear at all; but fortunately, here, the sun is prevailing.

Murnau und das blaue Land

Das berühmte Malerpaar, die Berlinerin Gabriele Münter und der Moskauer Wassily Kandinsky, wussten schon, warum sie sich im Jahre 1908 in Murnau niederließen. Geformt wurde dieses wunderschöne Land vom Loisachgletscher, der ein breites Tal zwischen Ester- und Ammergebirge ausschürfte. Jenseits der Anhöhe, auf der Murnau liegt, hatte er noch die Kraft, zwei weitere Gletscherbecken auszuformen, die den Staffelsee und den Riegsee bilden.

Der sieben Quadratkilometer große Staffelsee mit seinen sieben grünen Inseln und vielen kleinen Buchten zählt zu den Perlen der oberbayerischen Seen. Die Hauptinsel Wörth war schon in prähistorischer Zeit besiedelt. Vom 7. Jahrhundert an trug sie ein Kloster, vom 13. bis ins 18. Jahrhundert eine Kirche. Aus dieser Zeit hat sich im alten Fischerort Seehausen an Fronleichnam die Bootsprozession erhalten – die einzige in Bayern. Der kleine Bruder des Staffelsees, der Riegsee, liegt ein Stückchen weiter nordöstlich. Von nirgendwo sonst hat man einen schöneren Blick auf das mächtige Zugspitzmassiv.

Unweit seines Nordufers erhebt sich die Aidlinger Höhe auf 800 Meter. Der Aufstieg wird an klaren Tagen mit einem phantastischen Blick über das Wasser- und Hügelland auf die Bergkette der bayerischen Alpen belohnt. Wer noch mehr Natur, Einsamkeit und Ruhe sucht, der muss ein Stück weiter Richtung Norden. Unweit von Iffeldorf liegt das Naturschutzgebiet der Osterseen mit seinen 21 größeren und kleineren Seen, die man auf einem Netz von Wanderwegen erkunden kann.

Zurück nach Murnau. Im Süden der Stadt erstreckt sich das Murnauer Moos, mit 3500 Hektar Ausdehnung die größte weitgehend unkultivierte und geschützte Moorfläche im Alpenraum. Das Moos weist alle Stadien der Moorbildung auf, wie Flachmoore, Übergangsmoore und Hochmoore. 1250 Pflanzenarten, darunter ca. 160, die anderorts selten oder bereits ausgestorben sind, können dort noch bewundert werden. Etwa zwei Drittel aller Libellenarten Europas sind hier beheimatet. Bedrohte Vögel, wie der Wachtelkönig oder das Braunkehlchen, finden hier noch eine Heimat. Ausgangs- und Endpunkt aller Wanderungen ist das Ramsachkircherl im Norden des Moorgebiets, und auf den Wegen genießt man eine traumhafte Aussicht auf die Berge. Im Osten sind Heimgarten und Herzogstand zu sehen, im Süden die Hohe Kiste, Krottenkopf, Ettaler Mandl und Zugspitze, im Westen Aufacker und Hörnle.

Wer sich nach einem Spaziergang im Moos nach Kultur sehnt, der ist in wenigen Minuten in Murnau. Auf einem kleinen Hügel über dem Moorgebiet liegt der Ort, der bereits im 12. Jahrhundert beurkundet war und 1322 von Kaiser Ludwig von Bayern zum Markt erhoben wurde. Mehrere Brände haben die alte Stadt zerstört, doch zwischen 1906 und 1910 stellte der Architekt Emanuel von Seidl das alte Straßenbild wieder her. Murnau konnte sich das leisten – dank der Sommergäste, die nach dem Eisenbahnanschluss 1879 in Scharen anreisten. Seit den sechziger Jahren des 20. Jahrhunderts ist es nun in erster Linie ein Moorkurbad.

Berühmt wurde Murnau aber durch seine »Zuagroasten«: die Berlinerin Gabriele Münter und den Moskauer Wassily Kandinsky. Das Paar ließ sich 1908 in Murnau nieder und gründete 1911 zusammen mit Franz Marc sowie August und Elisabeth Macke die Künstlervereinigung »Der blaue Reiter«. Das »Russenhaus« wurde bald zum Anlaufpunkt einer Vielzahl von Künstlern, doch der Erste Weltkrieg zerstörte die Idylle. Münter kehrte 1931 zusammen mit dem Kunsthistoriker Johannes Eichner wieder zurück und vermachte das Anwesen noch vor ihrem Tod der Städtischen Galerie München.

Pferde des Bayerischen Haupt- und Landgestütes Schwaiganger
Horses of the main Bavarian country stud, Schwaiganger

Murnau and the Blue Land

The famous artist couple, Gabriele Münter of Berlin and Vassily Kandinsky of Moscow, knew very well why they took up residence in Murnau in 1908. This lovely area was formed by the Loisach glacier, which slurped a wide valley between the Ester and Ammer mountains. On the other side of the elevation on which Murnau lies it had the strength to carve out two more glacial basins which form the Lake Staffelsee and Lake Riegsee.

The seven square-kilometer Lake Staffelsee with its seven green islands and many small bays is one of the pearls among the Bavarian lakes. There was a prehistoric settlement on the main island of Wörth and from the seventh century, a monastery, from the thirteenth to the eighteenth century, a church. Ever since then there has been a boat procession in the old fishing village of Seehausen on Corpus Christi, the only one of its kind in Bavaria. The western shore is a large nature conservation area that is very inviting for nature lovers to hike in. The small Lake Riegsee is situated a little farther north east. It has the most beautiful view towards the Zugspitze mountain.

Not far away from the north bank, the Aidlinger Höhe rises up to 800 m. On clear days if you climb up, you may be rewarded with a fantastic view over the hilly countryside towards the Bavarian Alps. Whoever is looking for even more nature, solitude and peace should turn a little farther north. Near Iffeldorf is the nature conservation area of the Easter Lakes (Osterseen) with 21 lakes of various sizes that can be explored from a network of hiking trails.

Returning to Murnau, south of the town lies the Murnau Moss which extends over 3,500 hectares and is the biggest, largly uncultivated and protected moorland area in the alpine region. The moor features all stages of the formation of marshland like fens, temporary and high moors. There are 1,250 plant varieties to be admired there, of which about 160 are rarely to be found elsewhere or have already died out. About one third of all types of European dragonflies are native here, endangered birds like the corncrake (crex crex) or the winchat (Saxicola rubetra) are still at home here. The starting point and end of every hike is the Ramsachkircherl in the north of the moorland and along the trails one can enjoy a wonderful view of the mountains. Heimgarten and Herzogstand can be seen in the east, the Kiste, Krottenkopf, Ettaler Mandl and Zugspitze mountains in the south, Aufacker and Hornle in the west.

After a walk on the moors, Murnau is nearby if you are looking for culture. Situated on a hill above the marshland, Murnau was recorded in the twelfth century and elevated to a village in 1322 by Emperor Ludwig of Bavaria. The old town was destroyed by various fires, but between 1906 and 1910 it was reconstructed by the architect Emanuel von Seidl. Murnau was able to afford this thanks to the summer visitors who used to arrive in swarms after the railway was extended in 1879. Since the 1960s Murnau has become a moorland spa.

However, Murnau became famous for its newcomers – Gabriele Münter from Berlin and Vasily Kandinsky from Moscow – who settled there in 1908 and founded, together with Franz Marc and August and Elisabeth Macke, the artists' association "Der blaue Reiter" (The Blue Rider) in 1911. Many artists used to gather at the "Russenhaus", but the idyll was ruined by the onset of the First World War. Gabriele Münter returned there in 1931 with the art historian Johannes Eichner, and before her death she bequeathed the property to the Municipal Gallery of Munich.

In der Fußgängerzone von Murnau
Pedestrian zone in Murnau

Morgennebel am Riegsee
Morning mist over Lake Riegsee

Die ersten Sonnenstrahlen tauchen das Zugspitzmassiv in rotes
Licht. Im Vordergrund der nebelumhüllte Riegsee
The first rays of sun bathe the Zugspitz mountain in red. In the
foreground, the Lake Riegsee is shrouded in mist. ➜

*»Traum«-Wintertag im Murnauer
Moos
Winter dream on the Murnau Moss*

Wesen aus einer anderen Welt? Nein, Strohdrischeln im Murnauer Moos
Beings from another world? No, straw heaps in Murnau Moss

Kleine Kapelle vor dunklem Gewitterhimmel am Riegsee
Dark, stormy sky with chapel at the Lake Riegsee

Für Naturliebhaber eine Oase: die Osterseen
Oasis for nature lovers: the Easter Lakes ➤

Das Ramsachkircherl am Rande des Murnauer Mooses
The little Ramsach church on the edge of Murnau Moss

Frühling im Murnauer Moos
Spring on the Murnau Moss

Ruderboote am Staffelsee
Rowing boats on the Lake Staffelsee ➜

Die Fronleichnamsprozession am Staffelsee ist die letzte »Bootprozession« (Seeprozession) in Bayern.
Corpus Christi procession at Lake Staffelsee is the last procession of its kind, by boat, in Bavaria.

Osterfeuer in Harbach
Easter bonfire in Harbach

Pfaffenwinkel pur – zwischen Ammer und Lech

Die Ammer, ein temperamentvoller Fluss, der im Ammergebirge entspringt, bahnt sich ihren Lauf durch höhlenreichen Bergmischwald. Im wilden Ammertal zwischen Unterammergau und Saulgrub liegen sie dann versteckt im Wald, nur über einen kleinen Steig zu erreichen: die Schleierfälle, eines der größten Naturwunder Oberbayerns. Aus mit Moosen überzogenen Felsen fließt das Wasser in seidenen Fäden hinab. Besonders im Frühling, wenn die Moose im schönsten Grün leuchten, lohnt ein Ausflug zu diesem verwunschenen Ort.

Unweit der Schleierfälle liegt die prachtvolle Rokoko-Wallfahrtskirche »auf der Wies«. Alles begann im Jahre 1738 mit dem weinenden Christus. Im Kämmerchen der Wiesbäuerin Maria Lori flossen dem Heiland Tränen über das Gesicht. Pilger aus ganz Bayern machten sich auf zu diesem wunderbaren Ort. Schon 1746 begannen die Brüder Zimmermann mit dem Bau der Wieskirche, die sie 1754 einweihten. Das Gotteshaus offenbart seinen Glanz allerdings erst, wenn man durch die Eingangstür schreitet. Im Inneren erwartet den Besucher ein vollkommener Rokokoraum. Das Deckenfresko mit einer Darstellung des jüngsten Gerichts ist das Glanzstück in einem Gesamtkunstwerk, das von der UNESCO zum Weltkulturerbe erklärt wurde.

Ein Stück weiter nördlich lädt die ehemalige Klosterkirche Rottenbuch zu einem Besuch ein. 1073 hat sie Welf I. für den Orden der Augustinerchorherren gestiftet. Joseph und Franz Xaver Schmuzer gestalteten das Kloster in den Jahren 1737 bis 1746 im Baustil des Barock und Rokoko neu.

Fährt man von Rottenbuch weiter nach Norden, gelangt man nach Peiting, im Mittelalter Stammburg der Welfenherzöge. Gegenüber entstand um 1200 am linken Lechufer

Löwenzahnwiese vor dem Kircherl bei Raisting
Dandelion meadow in front of the church at Raisting

die Siedlung Schongau. Schon nach dreißig Jahren verlegten die Bewohner ihre Stadt auf einen drei Kilometer entfernten Hügel und gründeten ein neues Schongau. Aus dem alten Schongau wurde das Dorf »Altenstadt«. Schongaus Herz schlägt heute am Marienplatz. Hier dominieren das Ballenhaus (1419 erbaut) auf der einen Seite und die Stadtpfarrkirche Mariä Himmelfahrt auf der anderen Seite des Platzes. Auch die weitgehend erhaltene Stadtmauer stellt eine Attraktion dar.

Nur wenige Kilometer weiter östlich treffen wir wieder auf ein kulturelles Zentrum. Weilheim galt vom 16. bis 18. Jahrhundert als Talentschmiede für Bildhauer. Man sprach sogar von einer Weilheimer Bildhauerschule. Hans Krumper, Hans Degler, Bartholomäus Steinle und Franz Xaver Schmädl gingen daraus hervor. Von Weilheim ist es nur ein Katzensprung bis Wessobrunn. Hier geht es ein wenig beschaulicher zu als im geschäftigen Weilheim. Wiederum bildet ein Kloster den Kern des Ortes. Kloster Wessobrunn wurde schon 753 von Herzog Tassilo gegründet. Von der zwischen 1680 und 1730 von Johann Schmuzer und seinen Söhnen gebauten Neuanlage des ehemaligen Benediktinerklosters hat die Säkularisation nur wenige Trakte übrig gelassen. Berühmt war Wessobrunn für die Kunst des Stuckierens, und die Kirchen des Pfaffenwinkels sind ein wahres Musterbuch des Wessobrunner Stucks. Auch im Kloster selbst können heute noch wahre Glanzstücke der Stuckkunst bewundert werden.

Wir fahren weiter Richtung Norden und erreichen alsbald das nördliche Tor zum Pfaffenwinkel – Landsberg am Lech. Die Stadt verdankt ihren zeitweise beachtlichen Wohlstand ihrer Lage an der Salzstraße. Noch heute glänzt sie mit perfekt erhaltenen, farbigen Bürgerhäusern, dem dreieckigen Marktplatz, dem barocken Rathaus und einer wunderschön verwinkelten Altstadt mit vielen kleinen und schmalen Gassen.

Pfaffenwinkel, between the Ammer and Lech Rivers

The Ammer is a lively river, originating in the Ammer mountain range, that fights its way down through the mixed forest of the mountain. In the wild Ammer valley between Unterammergau and Saulgrub, hidden in the forest, only reachable up a small steep track, is one of the greatest wonders of nature in Upper Bavaria – the Schleier Falls – where the water flows in silky threads down mossy cliffs. In spring, when the moss is at its greenest and shiniest, it is well worth visiting this enchanting place.

Not far away from the Schleier Falls is the splendid rococo pilgrimage Church on the Meadow ("auf der Wiese"), which goes back to 1738 and the weeping Christ. The figure of the Saviour in the room of Maria Lori, a local peasant, began to shed tears and pilgrims from all over Bavaria came flocking. In 1746 the Zimmerman brothers started building the Meadow Church which was dedicated in 1754. One must enter the church to see its full splendour and rococo perfection. The fantastic ceiling fresco of the Final Judgement is the crowning glory of the whole work of art which has been declared world cultural heritage by UNESCO.

A little further north, the former monastery church of Rottenbuch is worth a visit. It was founded in 1073 by Welf I for the Order of Augustine Canons. From 1737 to 1746 Joseph and Xaver Schmuzer remodeled the monastery in the baroque and rococo architectural style.

Going north from Rottenbuch you get to Peiting, which was the family seat of the Welfen dukes in the Middle Ages. Opposite, on the left side of the Lech, the settlement of Schongau emerged around 1200. After about 30 years the inhabitants moved their town to a hill three kilometers away and founded a new Schongau. The old Schongau became the village of "Altenstadt". The heart of Schongau is its Marienplatz (St. Mary's Square) with Ballenhaus on one side (built in 1419) and the parish Church of the Dormition of the Virgin Mary on the other side of the square. The city wall is largely preserved and also of interest; if you would like to see it from above, a trip up the Hohenpeißenberg is to be recommended.

A few kilometers farther east is another cultural centre. From the 16th to the 18th centuries Weilheim was considered a place where sculptors could forge their talent. One spoke of the Weilheim School of Sculpture. Hans Krumper, Hans Degler, Bartholomäus Steinle and Franz Xaver Schmädl emanated from there. It is only a stone's throw from Weilheim to Wessobrunn, where it is a little more contemplative than in busy Weilheim. Once more a monastery is the heart of the place: Wessobrunn Monastery was founded in 753 by Duke Tassilo. A new annex was added between 1680 and 1730 by Johann Schmuzer and his sons, but secularisation has left only a few wings of the former Benedictine monastery remaining. Wessobrunn was famous for the art of stucco and the churches of Pfaffenwinkel are classic examples of Wessobrunn stucco work. Some fine specimens of the art are also to be admired in the Monastery itself.

Travelling north we soon reach Landsberg at the Lech, the northern gate of Pfaffenwinkel. This town owes its intermittent considerable prosperity to its location on the Salt Route and still boasts perfectly preserved coloured town houses, a triangular marketplace, a baroque townhall and a wonderful old town centre with many winding, narrow little streets.

Hell erleuchtet: Die Kirche von Wildsteig, im Hintergrund die Tannheimer Kette
Shining brightly – the Wildsteig church with the Tannheimer chain as a backdrop

Blick vom Hohenpeißenberg über das nebelverhangene Alpenvorland auf die Bayerischen Alpen
View of Hohenpeißenberg over the foggy foothills of the Bavarian Alps

Vom Hirschberg bei Pöhl schaut man auf die Allgäuer Alpen.
View of Hirschberg over the Allgaeu Alps ➜

Kloster Wessobrunn
Wessobrunn Monastery

In der Innenstadt von Schongau
Downtown Schongau

Die Kirche »auf der Wies« oder Wies-
kirche
The Meadow Church

Landsberg am Lech im äußersten Nord-
westen des Pfaffenwinkels
Landsberg at the Lech in the north west
corner of Pfaffenwinkel

Die Schleierfälle in der Ammerschlucht
Schleierfälle (waterfall) in the Ammer Gorge

Wegekreuz nahe Wessobrunn
Wayside cross near Wessobrunn

Was sagt er? Unterhaltung auf dem Kaltfohlenmarkt in Rottenbach
Conversing at the Market in Rottenbach

Oberbayerische Wadeln
Bavarian legs

Auf dem Kaltfohlenmarkt in Rottenbach
More scenes from the market at Rottenbach

← Blick über Weilheim hinweg auf die Ammergauer Alpen
View towards Weilheim and beyond to the Ammergau Alps

Die Satellitenschüsseln bei Raisting wirken in der Dämmerung wie
Wesen aus einer anderen Welt.
Satellite dishes in the twilight near Raisting resemble beings from
outer space.

Der Starnberger See – Perle unter Bayerns Seen

Schmal und elegant südwärts gestreckt liegt der Starnberger See inmitten der oberbayerischen Moränenhügellandschaft. Der von Gletschern geschaffene See ist mit 57 Quadratkilometern Fläche nach dem Chiemsee das zweitgrößte Gewässer Bayerns. An klaren Tagen, oder wenn der Föhn warm von den Bergen weht, entfaltet er seine wahre Magie, denn dann sind die Berge zum Greifen nahe. Dieser See hat mehrere Namen. Früher hieß er »Würmsee« nach der im Norden abfließenden Würm, und im 16./17. Jahrhundert wurde er zuweilen spöttisch als »Fürstensee« bezeichnet, weil schon damals der Adel das Land um den See für sich entdeckte. Angelockt von den schönen Bildern der um 1800 einsetzenden Landschaftsmalerei, kamen im 19. Jahrhundert auch die Münchner Bürger, und als 1851 die Dampfschifffahrt am See und 1854 die Eisenbahnlinie Pasing – Starnberg eröffnet wurde, gab es kein Halten mehr.

Die landschaftsgebundene Bebauung des 19. und frühen 20. Jahrhunderts schuf jene architektonische Vielfalt an den Ufern, für die der See auch heute noch berühmt ist. In der zweiten Hälfte des vergangenen Jahrhunderts wurden leider viele Uferstreifen privatisiert, doch zum Glück gibt es die beiden großen öffentlichen Bade- und Erholungsgelände in Possenhofen und St. Heinrich. Ergänzt werden diese beiden frei zugänglichen Ufergebiete durch 14 kleinere Strandbäder rund um den See. Für Wanderlustige wurde ein 48 Kilometer langer Rundweg eingerichtet, die Radltour ist vier Kilometer länger. Die schönste Art, den See zu erkunden, ist jedoch eine Schiffsrundfahrt. Die Fahrt dauert drei Stunden und bietet häufig die einzige Möglichkeit, einen Blick auf die Ufervillen zu werfen.

Das ehemalige Fischer- und Bauerndorf Starnberg, München am nächsten, war der erste Ort, den sich die Großstädter als Villendomizil erkoren. Das prächtige Holzbauernhaus aus dem 16. Jahrhundert in der Possenhofer Str. 5, heute Heimatmuseum, zählt zu den wenigen Sehenswürdigkeiten.

Am Westufer reihen sich die Villenkolonien aneinander. Niederpöcking, Possenhofen, Feldafing. Erwähnenswert ist hier vor allem die Roseninsel, die König Max II. gartenkünstlerisch gestalten ließ. Ein wenig weiter im Süden liegt Tutzing mit seinem 450 Jahre alten Schloss, heute der zweitgrößte Ort am See – und der eleganteste. Schöne Parks wechseln mit schattigen Alleen. Ein Spaziergang im Karpfenwinkel entlang der Schilfzone oder eine Wanderung auf die 728 Meter hohe Ilkahöhe gehören zu den schönsten Naturerlebnissen am Starnberger See.

Ursprünglicher geht es da schon in Bernried zu. Der Ort gehört zu den schönsten am ganzen See. Wundervolle alte Holzhäuser, im Sommer geschmückt mit prächtigen Balkonbepflanzungen, sind hier zu bewundern. Viele kommen aber wegen des im Jahre 2001 eröffneten »Museums der Phantasie« des Feldafinger Kunstsammlers Lothar-Günther Buchheim, das in einem eigenwilligen Bau eine der bedeutendsten Sammlungen deutscher Expressionisten beherbergt.

Da die Eisenbahnlinie zuerst das Westufer erschloss, blieb das Ostufer des Sees längere Zeit unangetastet. Ein bescheideneres Publikum ließ sich hier nieder – Ärzte, Architekten, Hofräte und Künstler. Dort liegt auch die Rottmannshöhe, die wie die Ilkahöhe zu den schönsten Aussichtspunkten am See gehört. Unweit von hier, in Berg, fand der berühmteste Bayer sein geheimnisvolles Ende. Am 13. Juni 1886, einem verregneten Pfingstsonntag, unternahm König Ludwig II. mit seinem Leibarzt Bernhard von Gudden einen Spaziergang an den See. Später fand man beide tot im Wasser. Das rätselhafte Geschehen gibt heute noch Anlass zur Spekulation. Ein Kreuz im See erinnert an den sagenumwobenen Märchenkönig.

Sonnenaufgang über dem Starnberger See bei Seeseiten
Sunrise over Lake Starnberg near Seeseiten

Lake Starnberg – Bavaria's jewel of a lake

In the midst of the Upper Bavarian morainic countryside, the Lake Starnberg elegantly stretches towards the south. Created from glaciers and with 57 square kilometers, it is the second largest lake in Bavaria after the Lake Chiemsee. On clear days or when the warm Foehn wind is blowing from the mountains, its true magic unfolds, because then the mountains seem near enough to touch. This lake has had several names: in the past it was called Lake Wurm after the north-flowing river Wurm, and in the 16th and 17th centuries it was sometimes called derisively "Princes' Lake", because even then the aristocracy had discovered the land around the lake for themselves. Attracted by beautiful landscape paintings popular around 1800, citizens of Munich began to arrive in the 19th century. With the steamer excursions from 1851 and the opening of the Pasing-Starnberg railway line in 1854, there was no stopping them.

Even today the lake is famous for the fact that the building development of the 19th and early 20th centuries along its shores created an architectural variety closely connected with the landscape. In the second half of the last century, many stretches of the shore were unfortunately privatised, but at least there are still the large public bathing and recreation areas in Possenhofen and St. Heinrich. These two open access places are supplemented by 14 smaller swimming areas around the lake. For those who like hiking there is a 48 km trail and the bicycle path is 4 km longer. The nicest way to get to know the lake however is by boat. Three times a day the boats set off from Starnberg and the three-hour excursion is often the only way to have a look at the chic villas along the shore.

The former fishing and farming village of Starnberg, on the side nearest to Munich, was the first place chosen by the city people for their villas. The splendid 16th century wooden farmhouse at number 5 Possenhofener Street, is today the Museum of Local History and one of the few places of interest.

The villa colonies are strung together on the western shore – Niederpocking, Possenhofen, Feldafing. Of chief interest here is the Rose Island which King Max II had designed as gardens. Tutzing lies a little farther south and with its 450 year-old palace, is the second largest town on the lake and the most elegant. Beautiful parks alternate with shady avenues. A walk in Karpfenwinkel along the reeds area or a hike up the 728 metre-high Ilkahohe are among the finest experiences of nature on Lake Starnberg.

Bernried is one of the loveliest and most natural places on the whole lake. The wonderful old wooden houses are much admired in summer for their marvellously decorated balconies. Many come to visit the "Museum of Fantasy" of the Feldafing art collector Lothar-Gunther Buchheim. This idiosyncratic building, which was opened in 2001, houses one of the most important collections of German Expressionists.

Since the railway line first of all opened up the western shore, the eastern side was untouched for a long time. A more unassuming set of people made there homes here: doctors, architects, councellors and artists. On that side is the Rottmannshohe, which like the Ilkahohe, is one of the best vantage points of the lake. The most famous Bavarian, King Ludwig II, met his mysterious end nearby, in Berg. On June 13, 1886, a rainy Whit Sunday, Ludwig was taking a walk at the lake with Bernhard von Gudden, his personal physician. Later they were both found dead in the water. Even today this puzzle is cause for speculation. The legendary fairy-tale king is commemorated by a cross in the lake.

»Bayerische Adria« – so der Spitzname für das öffentliche Naherholungsgelände nahe St. Heinrich
"Bavarian riviera" , recreational area near St. Heinrich

← »Ihn« kennt jeder, den Baum bei Münsing, direkt an der Autobahn.
Everybody knows The Tree on the highway at Muensing.

Eine Lichtstimmung mit Seltenheitswert, der Baum bei Münsing
vor den Ammergauer Alpen
The Tree in the foreground of the Ammergau Alps

Mond über der Kapelle von Degerndorf
Chapel at Degerndorf by night

*Sonnenuntergang über dem Starnberger
See bei St. Heinrich
Sunset over Lake Starnberg at St. Hein-
rich*

*Nach Sonnenuntergang entfaltet der
See seine ganze Magie.
After sunset the lake becomes magical.*

Zwei Schwäne präsentieren sich stolz an der Strandpromenade von Starnberg.
Two proud swans present themselves at the Starnberg promenade.

Ein prächtiges Exemplar in Starnberg an der Seepromenade
A fine specimen on the beach at Starnberg promenade

Mit dem Nachwuchs unterwegs
Out with their young

Kreuz zur Erinnerung an König Ludwig II., der hier seinen Tod fand.
Cross commemorating King Ludwig II who died here.

Badespaß in Ambach
Fun swimming at Ambach

Die zwei Löwen bei Tutzing wachen
über den See.
Two lions guard the lake at Tutzing.

Warten auf den Sonnenuntergang am Steg bei St. Heinrich
Waiting for sunset at the St. Heinrich jetty

Yachthafen bei Seeseiten
Marina at Seeseiten ➜

*Morgenrot über dem Starnberger
See, gesehen von der Ilkahöhe
Sunrise over Lake Starnberg, seen
from Ilkahohe →*

*Zu Maria Himmelfahrt werden
die Häuser in Bernried festlich
erleuchtet.
Houses in Bernried illuminated for
the celebration of the Feast of the
Dormition of the Virgin Mary*

*Maria-Himmelfahrts-Prozession in
Bernried
Dormition procession in Bernried*

Der Ammersee und seine Trabanten

Lediglich ein paar Kilometer voneinander getrennt und doch so verschieden sind die beiden großen Seen im Fünfseenland. Anders als der »Fürstensee« stand der gern als »Bauernsee« bezeichnete Ammersee jahrhundertelang unter dem Zeichen des Krummstabes. Die Eisenbahn erreichte ihn erst 1903, fünfzig Jahre später. Es dauerte deshalb ein wenig länger bis sich hier, natürlich in weitaus bescheidenerem Rahmen, private Villen am Ufer breit machten. Im Gegensatz zum Starnberger See ist die Verbauung geradezu bescheiden, und die Natur selbst hat dafür gesorgt. Der mit 47 Quadratkilometern Fläche drittgrößte See Bayerns ist im Norden und Süden von Mooren eingefasst und für eine Verbauung nicht geeignet. Hinzu kommt, dass heute fast das gesamte Westufer und Teile des Ostufers unter Landschaftsschutz stehen. Ganz im Süden, an der Mündung der Ammer in den See, liegt überdies ein Vogelschutzgebiet. So geht es am Ammersee ein wenig ruhiger und beschaulicher zu. Natürlich fahren auch dort die Schiffe der bayerischen Seenschifffahrt, und es kommt geradezu einem nostalgischen Abenteuer gleich, wenn man sich mit dem alten Schaufelraddampfer »Dießen« über den See schippern lässt.

Im Nordosten liegen drei kleine Seen, die sich wie Trabanten um den Ammersee gruppieren: der Wörthsee, ein überaus beliebter Badesee, mit dem schönen Hauptort Steinebach, der Pilsensee zu Füßen von Schloss Seefeld und der winzige Weßlinger See. Zusammen mit den beiden großen Seen bilden sie die »Kernzone« des Fünfseenlandes, die im Osten überragt wird vom »Heiligen Berg«, auf dem Kloster Andechs thront. Weithin sichtbar ragt der Turm des Klosters über die hügelige Landschaft des Alpenvorlandes. 1388 fand

Kloster Andechs im Wintergewand
Andechs Monastery in winter dress

man hier die vom uralten Adelsgeschlecht der Andechser im Heiligen Land gesammelten Reliquien, und so entstand ein Wallfahrtsziel. Die Wittelsbacher errichteten auf dem »Heiligen Berg« um 1430 eine gotische Kirche, die 1455 in ein Benediktinerkloster umgewandelt wurde. Im selben Jahr zählte man in Andechs bereits 40 000 Pilger und das Kloster begann, Bier zu brauen. Heute werden in der hochmodernen Andechser Klosterbrauerei pro Jahr 80 000 Hektoliter Bier gebraut. Mehr als eine Million Gäste besuchen das gemütliche Bräustüberl, den Biergarten und den gepflegten Klostergasthof. Berühmt ist die Brauerei für ihr Starkbier, den hellen »Bergbock« und den dunklen »Doppelbock«, die beide weit über Andechs hinaus einen fast schon legendären Ruf genießen. Bei einem Alkoholgehalt von sieben Prozent ist freilich schon mancher Gast den Heiligen Berg eher heruntergestolpert als gestiegen.

Mit einer berühmten Klosterbrauerei kann das Marienmünster in Dießen, auf der anderen Seite des Sees, nicht aufwarten. In Sachen Pracht und Eleganz braucht das Kloster jedoch keinen Vergleich zu scheuen. Allein der »Dießener Himmel«, ein Deckenfresko, das 28 Heilige und Selige aus dem Geschlecht der Andechs-Meranier zeigt, gehört zu den schönsten Kunstwerken im ganzen Pfaffenwinkel. Den besten Blick auf Dießen und sein Kloster hat man vom Ostufer des Ammersees. Wuchtig und erhaben thront das Kloster hier über dem Ort.

Ein Stück weiter südlich, beim Dorf Raisting, glänzen zehn riesige Metallschüsseln und eine große weiße Kugel in der Sonne, mittendrin das St.-Johannes-Kirchlein. Es handelt sich um die 1963 eingerichtete Satelliten-Funkstation. Von im Weltall kreisenden Nachrichtensatelliten werden hier Daten empfangen. Eine Tonbildschau in der Halbkugel »Radom« informiert umfassend über das ganze Projekt.

The Lake Ammersee and its 'satellites'

They are only a few kilometres away from each other yet the two large lakes of the Five Lakes region are so different. Unlike the "Princes' Lake", the Lake Ammersee was designated the "Farmers' Lake" and for hundreds of years came under the sign of the shepherd's crook. The railway connection to this lake arrived 50 years later, in 1903, and it took a little longer before private villas on the shores became popular, on a more modest scale of course. Contrary to Lake Starnberg, the development here is virtually unassuming, thanks also to nature itself. The third largest Bavarian lake, with 47 square kilometres, is enclosed by moorland in the north and south and not suitable for building construction. Furthermore, almost the whole of the western shore and parts of the eastern shore are under protection today. In the very south at the estuary of the river Ammer there is also a bird sanctuary. Thus, on the Lake Ammersee it is quieter and more contemplative. It is a paradise for yachtsmen with its many sailing schools and harbours. Of course the Bavarian Lake Excursion company has boats, too, and it is quite a nostalgic adventure to take a trip on the lake with the old paddle steamer "Dießen".

In the north east there are three smaller lakes that group around the Lake Ammersee like satellites: Lake Worthsee, extremely popular for bathing with its main place being Steinebach, Lake Pilsen at the foot of Seefeld Castle and tiny Lake Wessling. Altogether they form the core zone of the Five Lakes region, to the east of which towers the 'Holy Mountain' on which Andechs Monastery is enthroned. The monastery spire can be seen from far away over the foothills of the Alps. In 1388 relics were found which had been collected in the Holy Land by the ancient noble House of Andechs, and thus a place of pilgrimage emerged. Around 1430 the House of Wittelsbach built a gothic church on the 'Holy Mountain' and it became a Benedictine monastery. In the same year about 40,000 pilgrims came and the monks began to brew beer. Nowadays the highly modern Andechs Monastery Brewery produces 80,000 hectolitres of beer per year and more than a million people visit the pub, the beer garden and the very nice inn. The brewery is famous for its strong beer brew – 'Starkbier', as well as the light-coloured 'Bergbock' and the dark 'Doppelbock' which have an almost legendary reputation far beyond Andechs. With an alcohol content of 7% it is obvious that some customers have stumbled rather than climbed down the Holy Mountain!

On the other side of the lake at Dießen, the Minster of St. Mary cannot come up with a famous brewery. As far as magnificence and elegance is concerned, the monastery need not be shy of comparison. The ceiling fresco alone, known as the 'Dießen Heaven', with its 28 saints and beatified members of the House of Andechs-Meranier, is one of the finest art works in all of Pfaffenwinkel. The best view of Dießen and its monastery is to be had from the eastern shore of the Lake Ammersee. The monastery looks massive and lofty enthroned up above the town.

A little further south, near Raisting Village, ten enormous metal dishes and a great white sphere gleam in the sun, in the midst of which is St. John's Church. This is the satellite communication station set up in 1963 where data is received from news satellites in orbit round the Earth. A sound slide show in the 'Radom' dish gives comprehensive information about the whole project.

Kirchturm und Maibaum – Oberbayern
per excellence in Egling
Church tower and maypole – real
Bavaria in Egling

Sonnenaufgang über dem winterlichen Ammersee
Sunrise in winter at Lake Ammersee ➔

Sonnenaufgang über dem Ammersee bei Dießen
Sunrise over the Lake Ammersee at Dießen

Morgendämmerung über dem Ammersee, rechts schaut das Kloster Andechs hervor.
Dawn over Lake Ammersee with Andechs Monastery visible to the right

← *Die letzten Sonnenstrahlen werden noch mal genossen, wie hier am Wörthsee.*
The last rays of sun enjoyed here on Lake Worthsee

Bootshäuser in Dießen am Ammersee
Boathouses in Diessen at Lake Ammersee

Vollmond über Kloster Dießen
Full moon over Diessen Monastery

Die Ruhe vor dem Sturm am Pilsensee
Calm before the storm at Lake Pilsen

Hoffentlich beißt einer an! Fischer am Pilsensee
Hopeful anglers at Lake Pilsen

Herbst am Weßlinger See, dem Winzling im Fünfseenland
Autumn at Lake Wessling, the smallest of the Five Lakes

Der Frühling ist endlich da! Löwen-
zahnwiese vor dem Ort Raisting
Spring at last! Dandelion field near
Raisting →

Wer hat die schönsten Fenster? Ich oder
die Nachbarin?
Whose is the most beautiful, mine or the
neighbour's?

← *Es war ein guter Fang! Ammerseefischer beim Einholen der Fische*
A good catch! Fisherman hauling in the nets at Lake Ammersee

Nostalgie pur: Der Schaufelraddampfer »Dießen« fährt noch auf dem Ammersee.
Nostalgic paddle steamer 'Diessen' still sails the Lake Ammersee.

A Schnapserl muaß sei! Frauen während des Leonhardi-Ritts in Benediktbeuern
Down the hatch! Women at the St. Leonhard's celebration in Benediktbeuern

Besuchen Sie uns im Internet:
www.rosenheimer.com

© 2006 Rosenheimer Verlagshaus GmbH & Co. KG, Rosenheim

Englische Übersetzung: Suzanne Frank-Kilner, München
Karte: Sebastian Schrank, München
Seitenlayout und Satz: VerlagsService Dr. Helmut Neuberger
& Karl Schaumann GmbH, Heimstetten
Lithografie: Repro Ludwig, Zell am See
Druck und Bindung: Printer Trento S.r.l.
Printed in Italy

ISBN 3-475-53759-1